GREEN PLANET

GREEN BUILDINGS

by Rebecca Pettiford

Ideas for Parents and Teachers

Pogo Books let children practice reading informational text while introducing them to nonfiction features such as headings, labels, sidebars, maps, and diagrams, as well as a table of contents, glossary, and index.

Carefully leveled text with a strong photo match offers early fluent readers the support they need to succeed.

Before Reading

- "Walk" through the book and point out the various nonfiction features. Ask the student what purpose each feature serves.
- Look at the glossary together. Read and discuss the words.

Read the Book

- Have the child read the book independently.
- Invite him or her to list questions that arise from reading.

After Reading

- Discuss the child's questions. Talk about how he or she might find answers to those questions.
- Prompt the child to think more. Ask: Have you ever been in a green building? How was it different from other buildings?

Pogo Books are published by Jump!
5357 Penn Avenue South
Minneapolis, MN 55419
www.jumplibrary.com

Library of Congress Cataloging-in-Publication Data

Names: Pettiford, Rebecca, author.
Title: Green buildings / by Rebecca Pettiford.
Description: Minneapolis, MN: Jump!, Inc. [2016] Series: Green planet | Audience: Ages 7–10.
Includes bibliographical references and index.
Identifiers: LCCN 2016013595 (print)
LCCN 2016014177 (ebook)
ISBN 9781620314012 (hardcover: alk. paper)
ISBN 9781624964480 (ebook)
Subjects: LCSH: Sustainable buildings–Juvenile literature.
Sustainable architecture–Juvenile literature.
Classification: LCC TH880 .P4885 2016 (print)
LCC TH880 (ebook) | DDC 720.47–dc23LC record available at http://lccn.loc.gov/2016013595

Series Editor: Jenny Fretland VanVoorst
Series Designer: Anna Peterson
Book Designers: Anna Peterson and Leah Sanders
Photo Researcher: Kirsten Chang

Photo Credits: Alamy, 5, 14–15, 18; Dreamstime, 4; Eugenio Marongiu/Shutterstock.com, cover; Getty, 10–11; iStock, 12, 16–17; Shutterstock, 3, 6–7, 8, 9, 12–13, 19, 20–21, 23; yyama/Shutterstock.com, 1.

Printed in the United States of America at Corporate Graphics in North Mankato, Minnesota.

TABLE OF CONTENTS

CHAPTER 1

WHAT IS A GREEN BUILDING?

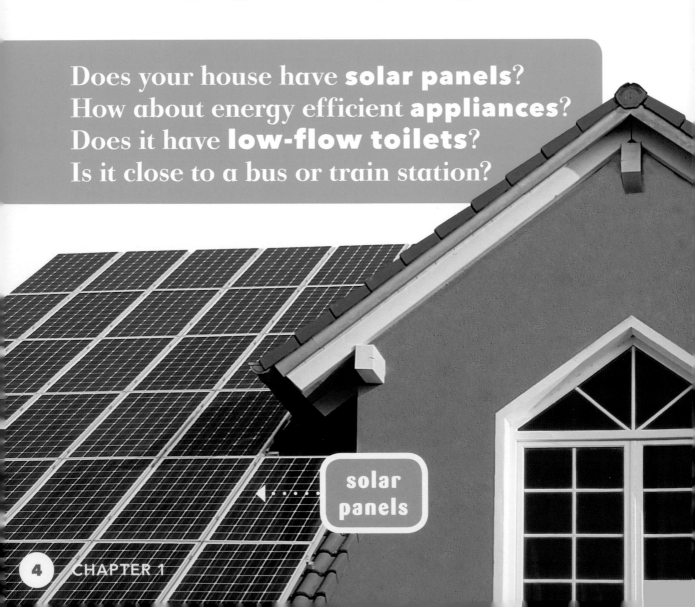

Does your house have **solar panels**? How about energy efficient **appliances**? Does it have **low-flow toilets**? Is it close to a bus or train station?

solar panels

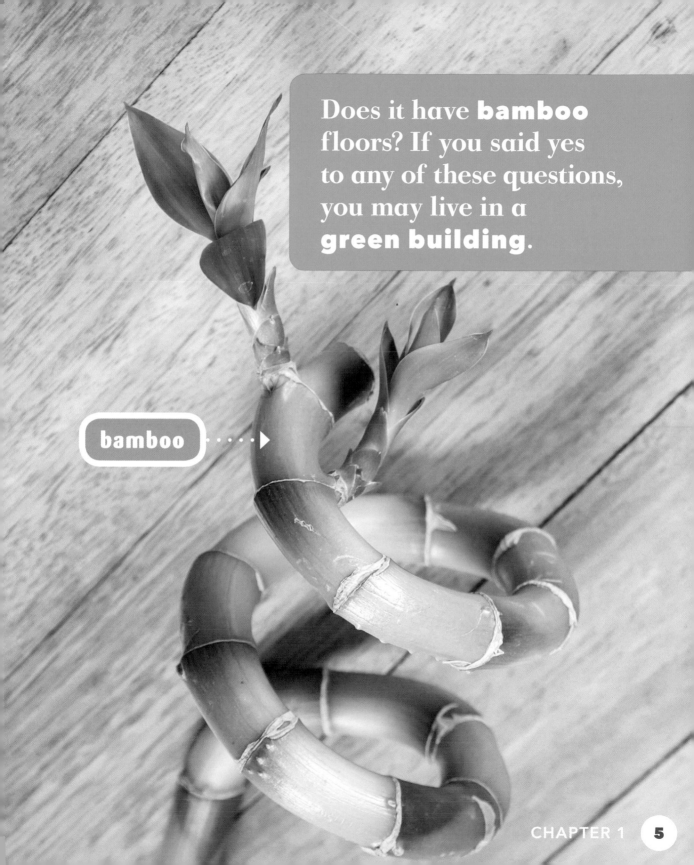

Does it have **bamboo** floors? If you said yes to any of these questions, you may live in a **green building**.

bamboo ·····▸

A green building works with nature. It makes the best use of energy, water, and other resources. This makes it **efficient**. It may cost more to build, but it saves money in energy. The air inside is cleaner, too. Research shows that people who live and work in green buildings stay healthier.

DID YOU KNOW?

Are your appliances energy efficient? Look for the ENERGY STAR sticker. These labels identify the most energy efficient devices.

CHAPTER 2

GREEN BUILDING BASICS

Burning fuel to create heat and electricity releases **greenhouse gases**. These are the gases that cause global warming. But green buildings use less energy. They create less greenhouse gas. How?

Windows that face the sun **capture** the sun's energy to warm the building.

Solar panels change sunlight into power. This gives the building electricity.

A **green roof** can save on heating and cooling costs. The plants on top act as **insulation**. Birds and other animals enjoy them, too.

A small **wind turbine** can go on the roof. It uses wind energy to help power the building.

Green buildings use less water, too. Low-flow toilets cut down on water use. The yards have plants that need less water. They can be watered with greywater. It is the used water from sinks and showers.

In Order to Conserve Water...

RECYCLED WATER
IN USE

DO NOT DRINK

NO TOME EL AGUA

WASH HANDS AFTER CONTACTING
LAVESE SUS MANOS DESPUES DE USAR

straw

Green buildings use **sustainable** products. These are used up at the same rate they return. Builders can use bamboo for floors. It is easy to grow, and it grows fast. They can use straw for insulation.

The act of building makes a lot of waste. To cut waste, builders use **recycled** products. Drywall waste becomes new drywall. Wood waste becomes **mulch** for the yard.

drywall
waste

wood
waste

TAKE A LOOK!

What are some things that can make a house greener?

1. Shade trees
2. Solar panels
3. Low-flow toilet
4. ENERGY STAR washer and dryer
5. Bamboo floor
6. LED light bulbs
7. ENERGY STAR kitchen appliances

CHAPTER 3

THE FUTURE IS GREEN

Greenhouse gases are warming the planet. Some parts of Earth do not get enough water. What can we do to save our planet for the future?

Building green can help.
It can reduce greenhouse gases.
It can cut water waste.

SURVIVE AT SEA WITH
THE U.S. NAVY SEALs

CHRIS McNAB

**Introduction by Colonel John T. Carney. Jr., USAF–Ret.
President, Special Operations Warrior Foundation**

MASON CREST PUBLISHERS

This edition first published in 2003
by Mason Crest Publishers Inc.
370 Reed Road, Broomall, PA, 19008

Library of Congress Cataloging-in-Publication Data available

ISBN 1-59084-006-2

Editorial and design by
Amber Books Ltd.
Bradley's Close
74–77 White Lion Street
London N1 9PF

Project Editor Chris Stone
Designer Simon Thompson
Picture Research Lisa Wren

Printed and bound in Malaysia

10 9 8 7 6 5 4 3 2 1

ACKNOWLEDGMENT
For authenticating this book, the Publishers would like to thank the Public Affairs Offices of the U.S. Special Operations Command, MacDill AFB, FL.; Army Special Operations Command, Fort Bragg, N.C.; Navy Special Warfare Command, Coronado, CA.; and the Air Force Special Operations Command, Hurlbert Field, FL.

IMPORTANT NOTICE
The survival techniques and information described in this publication are for use in dire circumstances where the safety of the individual is at risk. Accordingly, the publisher cannot accept any responsibility for any prosecution or proceedings brought or instituted against any person or body as a result of the uses or misuses of the techniques and information within.

DEDICATION
This book is dedicated to those who perished in the terrorist attacks of September 11, 2001, and to the Special Forces soldiers who continually serve to defend freedom.

Picture Credits
Corbis: 16, 20, 23, 34, 43, 46, 50, 54, 56, 58, 59, 63, 65, 74 ; **TRH**: 6, 11, 21, 24, 32, 33, 84, 86, 88; **/US Army**: 36; **/US Dept. of Defense**: 8, 17, 18, 39, 40, 44, 77, 78, 82; **/US Navy**: 12, 13, 14, 28, 30, 70
Illustrations courtesy of Amber Books, De Agostini UK and the following supplied by Patrick Mulrey: 79
Front cover: **Corbis** (both)

CONTENTS

INTRODUCTION

Elite forces are the tip of Freedom's spear. These small, special units are universally the first to engage, whether on reconnaissance missions into denied territory for larger, conventional forces or in direct action, surgical operations, preemptive strikes, retaliatory action, and hostage rescues. They lead the way in today's war on terrorism, the war on drugs, the war on transnational unrest, and in humanitarian operations as well as nation building. When large scale warfare erupts, they offer theater commanders a wide variety of unique, unconventional options.

Most such units are regionally oriented, acclimated to the culture and conversant in the languages of the areas where they operate. Since they deploy to those areas regularly, often for combined training exercises with indigenous forces, these elite units also serve as peacetime "global scouts" and "diplomacy multipliers," a beacon of hope for the democratic aspirations of oppressed peoples all over the globe.

Elite forces are truly "quiet professionals": their actions speak louder than words. They are self-motivated, self-confident, versatile, seasoned, mature individuals who rely on teamwork more than daring-do. Unfortunately, theirs is dangerous work. Since "Desert One"—the 1980 attempt to rescue hostages from the U.S. embassy in Tehran, for instance—American special operations forces have suffered casualties in real world operations at close to fifteen times the rate of U.S. conventional forces. By the very nature of the challenges which face special operations forces, training for these elite units has proven even more hazardous.

Thus it's with special pride that I join you in saluting the brave men and women who volunteer to serve in and support these magnificent units and who face such difficult challenges ahead.

Colonel John T. Carney, Jr., USAF–Ret.
President, Special Operations Warrior Foundation

SEAL commandos rush ashore with their breathing apparatus. SEALs training is so tough that the drop-out rate is over 65 percent.

THE U.S. NAVY SEALs

The U.S. Navy SEALs are the ultimate modern warriors. The name "SEALs" means Sea, Air, Land—the SEALs can fight in any environment. But they are best known for their ability to fight from and survive in the water.

The U.S. Navy SEAL teams were born to fight in the jungles and rivers of Vietnam. The first SEAL units, Teams One and Two, were commissioned by President John F. Kennedy on January 1, 1962. Their job was to provide the Navy with a special operations unit able to conduct undercover warfare, intelligence gathering, combat-rescue, and even missions to help the local Vietnamese population fight against the communist **Viet Cong** guerrillas. These two new teams became part of the Naval Special Warfare Groups. They were joined by the existing Underwater Demolition Teams (UDTs), which had seen action in World War II and the Korean War. The UDTs' special talents were beach reconnaissance and mine clearance, and they were strong and ruthless soldiers in battle.

As the Vietnam War intensified, the UDTs and SEALs were quickly sent to support the U.S. Navy fleet fighting in the canals, estuaries, and rivers of South Vietnam. This fleet was known as the "Brown Water Navy" because of the color of the water in Vietnam's rivers. The battle on these rivers was fierce. The Viet Cong used the

As all-round athletes, SEALs can swim with full kit for at least five miles (8 km) on the water's surface, and two miles (3.2 km) below.

rivers to supply their troops, and they had bases set in the jungle on the riverbanks. SEAL platoons disrupted the VC supply lines and camps along the many rivers, operating out of small, fast, armored riverboats laden with machine guns and rocket launchers. If the Viet Cong or the communist **North Vietnamese Army** (NVA) tried to move along the river, SEAL ambushes would explode into life, cutting down communist soldiers with heavy firepower and destroying their bases and boats. Using the river to move in and out of their positions, the SEALs conducted a number of combat-rescue missions under what was called the "Bright Light" program.

In 1970, a team of 15 SEALs and 19 Vietnamese militia stormed a camp in Laos, a country that neighbored South Vietnam, from which the communists operated. The team rescued 19 South Vietnamese prisoners of war (POWs). In another incident, an American SEAL and a Vietnamese soldier rescued Lieutenant-Colonel Hambleton when his electronic warfare plane, "Bat 21," was shot down in the Song Mieu Giang River area. In all, the SEALs rescued 15 POWs and killed some 800 enemy troops. They won many medals for their bravery. The medals included two Presidential Unit Citations, one Navy and one Meritorious Unit Commendation, and 852 personal awards, from the Medal of Honor to the Navy Achievement Medal. These awards made the SEALs one of the most decorated units in Vietnam.

SEALs also took part in the 1983 invasion of the island of Grenada. The government there had been overthrown, and the U.S. launched a mission to put the government back in its place and protect U.S. citizens living on Grenada. The mission was code-

A SEAL on patrol in Vietnam in 1968. During this conflict, SEAL
teams concentrated on disrupting the enemy's ability to move freely
in the river areas of south and west Saigon.

named Operation "Urgent Fury." SEAL units were used on the very first day of the invasion—October 25. Men of SEAL Team Four were given the task of rescuing the Governor-General and taking him to a **safe house**. Another SEAL unit was ordered to destroy the radio transmitter of Radio Free Grenada, which the enemy could use to send messages. On October 25, SEALs landed on Grenada at 2200 hours. (To avoid confusion, the army measures time according to the 24-hour clock, so 2200 hours is 10 P.M.) Unfortunately, they received poor information before the mission, and this meant that they were less successful than

SEALs are trained to operate in hostile enemy waters. They must be able to work in teams, pairs, or alone, and have the skill to approach or move away from the shore by swimming or with an inflatable boat.

SEALs are expert in counterinsurgency techniques, and are trained to use a variety of weapons, from shotguns to submachine guns. In 1983, SEAL platoons were at the forefront of the Grenada operation.

expected. The team sent to shut down the radio walked straight into an ambush, and two men were killed in a vicious gun battle. They were forced to evacuate, having failed to destroy the radio station. The SEALs sent to rescue the Governor-General also met with disaster. As soon as they arrived at Government House, they were surrounded and besieged by Grenadan People's Revolutionary Army (PRA) forces.

The situation was dangerous and the SEALs requested help. Despite the fact that antiaircraft units were in the area, two AH-1T Cobra helicopters were dispatched from a U.S. aircraft carrier. They flew into a storm of bullets and **flak** and were both shot down. Undeterred, Admiral Metcalf, commander of the American task force, ordered heavily armed A-7 aircraft to fly from U.S. aircraft carriers to relieve the SEALs. The aircraft pummeled the anti-aircraft batteries, but they did not kill all the soldiers around Government House. When night came on the October 25, the SEALs were still surrounded.

Admiral Metcalf decided to use U.S. Marines aboard the Landing Ship Tank (LST) *Manitowac* to rescue the SEALs. In the early hours of the 26th, a company of U.S. Marines stormed ashore at Grand Mal Bay, on the west coast of the island. Mounted on armored vehicles with heavy machine guns and supported by five M-60 tanks, they brushed aside the enemy and headed to the rescue.

During the Gulf War, SEAL platoons conducted maritime missions using inflatable boats fitted with a powerful outboard motor.

PERSONAL QUALITIES ESSENTIAL TO SURVIVAL

The U.S. Navy SEALs know from long experience what soldiers need to survive. They must have the ability to:
- Concentrate the mind
- Improvise
- Live in isolation
- Adapt to any situation
- Remain calm

Government House was secured at 0700 hours and the Governor-General was finally evacuated to the U.S. island of Guam.

In 1991 the Gulf War began when Iraq invaded the neighboring country of Kuwait and occupied it. The United Nations organized an international army to liberate Kuwait. The SEALs were right at the front of the action, conducting many different missions. These included daring undercover operations to inspect Iraqi-held beaches that might be used for possible U.S. Marines landing sites. They also conducted deception operations on Faylakah Island off the Kuwaiti coast. These missions were meant to fool the Iraqis into thinking that a large-scale attack was about to happen there. The Iraqi officers fell for it, and they took many troops away from the front lines—where they were needed—in order to defend against an attack that never came. On land, SEAL teams were also involved in the hunt for Iraqi **Scud** long-range surface-to-surface missiles (SSMs), which were being launched against Israel and Saudi Arabia. Long-range reconnaissance missions by SEAL units were responsible for finding the missiles. Once they had found them, they fixed their position using powerful laser beams. Allied bombing aircraft then dropped "**smart bombs**" and destroyed many Iraqi missiles. Other tasks involved working with British Special Air Service (SAS) teams and capturing high-ranking Iraqi officers. They also stole enemy aircraft and surface-to-air missile (SAM) systems so that the Allies could find out what they were facing. Overall, the efforts of the SEALs were a major contribution to the eventual Allied victory.

The SEALs' training is some of the hardest in the world. Because they are **amphibious** soldiers (trained to operate from the sea), much of their training involves exhausting survival exercises in the sea, in rivers, and in swimming pools. They experience the torments

For all operations, SEALs wear gear appropriate to the terrain—from traditional combat kit (above) to a diver's cold-water exposure suit.

In a standard training pool, SEALs learn how to rescue pilots of downed aircraft.

of "Hell Week," a tough seven-day period of almost no sleep, in which they are constantly in ice–cold waters. One special test during this period is called "drownproofing." The recruits are thrown into a large, deep swimming pool with their ankles and wrists tied together. In this situation, they must perform the following exercises: dive down to the bottom of the pool and come back up again for five minutes; stay afloat for 20 minutes; do underwater back flips for five minutes; retrieve a face mask from the bottom of the pool using only their teeth; and make a quick 100-yard (90-m) swim.

Such training is tough, but the soldiers who survive it are some of the best in the world at surviving at sea and in any waters. In this book the Navy SEALs will tell us their techniques.

SEAS, OCEANS, AND WEATHER

The sea shows no mercy when it comes to survival; your first mistake in a maritime emergency is likely to be your last. You must master every ocean survival technique in order to live in this unforgiving environment.

Around 71 percent of the Earth's surface is covered by water. It is therefore vital that you learn how to survive in this environment. Human beings' natural place is land, and that makes survival at sea for any length of time very difficult. In particular, finding drinking water and food are serious problems for the survivor at sea, though the other dangers that the sea poses to the survivor should not be underestimated. The SEALs know how to cope with them all.

First, the SEAL gets to know the environment he or she faces. The temperature of surface water in the ocean can range from 79°F (26°C) in tropical regions to 29.5°F (−1.4°C), the freezing point of seawater, in polar regions. Around 50 percent of total ocean water has temperatures between 29.5°F (−1.4°C) and 39°F (3.8°C).

But the conditions of the sea vary enormously with the weather. Around the poles in winter, there are violent storms characterized by snow, winds of up to 40 miles per hour (64 km/h), and temperatures as low as −122°F (−50°C). Storms in the Atlantic and Pacific

Although the ocean is cold and unforgiving, SEALs must be prepared to jump in from a helicopter, such as this Boeing CH-47 Chinook.

Even the strongest swimmers are in danger from ocean currents. SEALs are trained to recognize, and adapt to, the four main types of current: tidal, wind, littoral, and rip.

Oceans can result in waves higher than a three-storied house. In contrast, in some areas of the Atlantic, Pacific, and Indian Oceans, there are times and places where there are no surface winds at all. The sea in these conditions becomes incredibly still, with no wind to help you travel if your boat does not have a motor.

Waterspouts (the equivalent of tornadoes at sea) are common off the Atlantic and Gulf Coasts and along the coasts of China and Japan. Hurricanes and typhoons occur in the warm areas of all oceans during the summer and fall. They can last for up to two weeks.

Sailors and SEAL soldiers are very aware of signs that indicate which way the weather is likely to turn. Two good indicators are the wind and the clouds. By recognizing the direction and changes of wind, the types of cloud, and the likely weather they indicate, you can prepare better for either good or bad weather. In the summer, in particular, the land is warmer than the sea during the day, but it is colder than the sea at night.

Clouds can be incredibly useful for surviving at sea because they can tell you a lot about what type of weather is heading your way. (See the diagram on the next page). There are four main groups of clouds, categorized on the basis of height above the Earth: cirrus, cumulus, nimbus, and stratus. The first type is cirrus cloud. Usually about four miles (6 km) above the Earth, cirrus clouds are composed

Breaker waves can quickly drag a swimmer under the water. SEALs must observe the behavior of the waves and act accordingly.

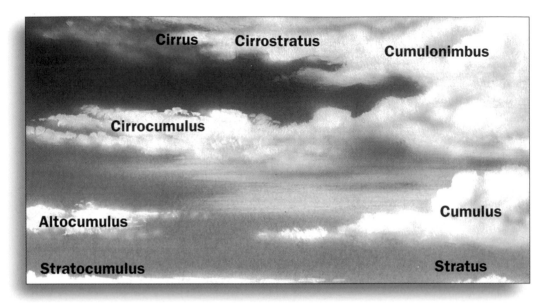

Recognizing the various cloud formations can indicate what type of weather is approaching, and the type of kit required for an operation.

of ice particles. They are feathery and long, and appear as streaky bands. They are known as **mare's tails**. These clouds can often indicate fine weather, but when they are accompanied by a regular north wind in cold climates, they sometimes precede a blizzard. Within cirrus comes cirrostratus and cirrocumulus. Cirrostratus consists of a fine veil of whitish clouds, darker than cirrus. When cirrostratus follows cirrus across the sky, bad weather may be about to arrive, so now is the time to make preparations. Cirrocumulus clouds give a different message. These clouds are small white balls arranged in groups, and they indicate good weather.

Next come cumulus clouds. Fluffy, white, and heaped together, these clouds are often indicators of fine weather. They can appear around midday on a sunny day. If they pile up and push higher into the **atmosphere**, they can become storm clouds. In the third

A huge spray of water crashes over the bows of this U.S. Navy ship on patrol in the Arctic Ocean. Smaller vessels, such as inflatable boats, might be capsized by large waves caused by bad weather.

Battered by ocean spray, two SEALs hang on to a rope connecting two ships during a rescue training exercise.

category, nimbus clouds paint the whole sky in a uniform gray color. This can mean bad weather, but it is even more serious if you see cumulonimbus. Towering into the atmosphere, these clouds are dark with flat bases and rounded tops. Sometimes they form an anvil shape at the top, looking like cirrus. They often mean sudden heavy showers of rain, snow, or hail. If a thunderstorm occurs, you can expect a strong wind from the direction of the storm as well as a rapid drop in temperature.

The final category is stratus. These are low clouds composed of water droplets that make up an even, gray layer of cloud. They inevitably mean rain or snow. Within stratus is altostratus. Holes in this layer mean that the weather may not be too bad. Finally comes nimbostratus. These rain-bearing clouds have a low base and consist of thick layers.

The clouds can tell you what the weather will be like, but you also need to be able to read the winds. A good way of doing this is using what is known as the Beaufort Scale. This scale helps you read how much danger you are in.

THE BEAUFORT SCALE

Description & wind speed (knots)	Land signs and sea signs
0 Calm (less than 1)	Smoke rises. Leaves do not stir.
1 Light air (1–3)	Smoke drifts, wind vanes are still.
2 Light breeze (4–6)	Wind felt on face. Vanes move. Rustling leaves.

3 Gentle breeze (7–10)	Light flags extended. Leaves in motion. Small waves (average wave height is 2 ft/60 cm).
4 Moderate breeze (11–16)	Small branches moving. Dust raised. Small waves, some with white crests (average wave height 3 ft 3 in/1 m).
5 Fresh breeze (17–21)	Small trees sway. Tops of trees move. White horses and spray off tops of waves (average wave height is 6 ft/1.8 m).
6 Strong breeze (22–27)	Large branches in motion. Whistling wires.
7 Near gale (28–33)	Trees in motion. Walkers buffeted. Seas piling up. Foam (average wave height is 13 ft/4 m).
8 Gale (34–40)	Twigs broken off trees. Difficult to walk.
9 Strong gale (41–47)	Slight structural damage. Shingles may blow away. Waves high with dense foam (average wave height is 23 ft/7 m).
10+ Storm (48+)	Trees are uprooted. Extremely high waves, large expanses of froth, edges of waves turned to foam (average wave height is 37 ft/11 m).

As soon as the wind reaches numbers 5 or 6 on this scale, you should head for safety if you are in a small boat at sea. The SEALs always need to know what weather is heading their way for their missions. But sometimes even they accept that disaster may strike.

THE WORLD'S OCEANS AND SEAS

The following chart lists the size of the world's oceans and sea in square miles. The Pacific Ocean is by far the biggest at almost 64 million square miles.

	Square miles	Square km
Arctic Ocean	5,426,000	14,056,000
Atlantic Ocean	31,736,000	82,217,000
Baltic Sea	163,000	422,000
Bering Sea	876,000	2,269,000
Black Sea	178,000	461,000
Caribbean Sea	750,000	1,943,000
East China Sea	482,000	1,248,000
Gulf of Mexico	596,000	1,544,000
Hudson Bay	476,000	1,233,300
Indian Ocean	28,364,000	73,481,000
Mediterranean Sea	967,000	2,505,000
North Sea	222,000	575,000
Pacific Ocean	63,838,000	165,384,000
Red Sea	169,000	438,000
Sea of Japan	389,000	1,008,000
Sea of Okhotsk	590,000	1,528,000
South China Sea	895,000	2,318,000
Yellow Sea	156,000	404,000

SWIMMING AND SURVIVAL

Being thrown into the sea can literally take your breath away. The SEALs teach you that in these situations there is no substitute for a clear and calm mind that helps you work out how to survive.

In survival circumstances, SEALs teach that it is better to retain clothing when in the water. If abandoning a ship or aircraft, take whatever warm clothing is available as well as easily portable food (chocolate and candies). Do not jump into the water with an inflated life jacket, because the impact may be dangerous.

Once in the water, inflate your life jacket, swim steadily, and look for any floating objects, such as pieces of wood, that will help you to keep afloat. Use a life raft if there is one around.

If you are escaping from a downed aircraft, swim or paddle upwind, especially if the plane is on fire. Remember, any large object, such as a plane or boat, will create suction when it sinks beneath the surface and can drag survivors down with it. Therefore, get away from the plane or boat as soon as possible.

If there is burning oil on the water, attempt to swim under it, using an underwater breaststroke. (You may need to deflate or throw away your life jacket for this.) When you need to come up for air, leave enough time to clear a space in the burning area by pushing the water aside from beneath the surface. Then take in enough

Before putting on their face masks, SEAL divers spit into the mask, then wash it out. This stops the mask fogging up in the water.

Swimming in the ocean for long periods is extremely tiring, especially if the water is cold. Floating on your back can provide much needed rest and ensure your head stays clear of the water.

breath and, if possible, look to check the shortest route to clear water before submerging again, straight downward, feet first.

Once clear of immediate danger, practice relaxing by floating on your back with your face above the water. This will let you gather your energy before swimming again to the nearest life raft or large floating object. If no life raft is available, but you are wearing a life jacket, adopt the Heat Escaping Lessing Posture (**HELP**) to keep as much body warmth as possible. The principle of HELP is keeping the head clear of the water, since most heat is lost through the head and neck.

If you have nothing to help you stay afloat, you can save energy by relaxing into a crouching position, which will let your body float just below the surface of the water, and then move your arms to bring your head up to the surface to breathe before relaxing into the crouch position again. However, these measures are only

In emergencies, the Heat Escaping Lessing Position (HELP) retains body heat, although, ideally, a wet suit or dry suit should be worn.

temporary—you must get out of the water. If you do not, you could quickly freeze to death.

If you are lucky, you might have found your way into a life raft. When in a raft, the SEALs' immediate priorities are rescue, protection from the elements, and water to drink. Obey the following rules: Give first aid to any wounded survivors. Check that any signaling equipment is ready to use. This may include flares, emergency radio, and flags. Save batteries of signaling equipment by using them only when search aircraft or ships are in range. Salvage any useful material that may be floating nearby. (It can be tied to

In icy conditions, an exposure suit and protective mittens maximizes the amount of time a SEAL can survive in cold water.

If their boat overturns, SEALs may ignite their emergency flares to attract attention, using the day or night signal as necessary.

the **dinghy** to provide more space inside.) Ensure that one member of the crew is attached to the life raft with a line, in case it tips over and is blown away. If you have supplies of drinking water, do not drink it all at once—ration it out. Check available supplies of food.

Follow the survival instructions you find on the life raft. Remove wet clothing when you can, and dry it out. In a cold climate, huddle together to share warmth. In a hot climate, keep at least one layer of clothing on to protect the body from the direct powerful light and heat of the sun. If any survivors have dry clothes, they should share

During a rescue operation, SEALs must work together to ensure the drowning person does not panic or struggle, thereby overturning their boat or dragging them into the water.

them with those who are wet. Those who are wet should be given the most sheltered positions in the raft, and they should be allowed to warm their hands and feet against those who are dry. If possible, give extra water rations to those suffering from cold **exposure**. You should exercise fingers, toes, legs, arms, shoulders, and buttocks to help keep you fit and strong. In a sitting position, put your hands under your armpits and raise your feet slightly off the ground. Keep them up for a minute or two. Try to exercise at least twice a day.

These actions should help you survive. But your goal is to be seen or to find safety. Your chances of being found are greatest if you are close to the area where rescuers were last in radio contact. Stay in the area for at least 72 hours to give them a chance to find you. The following actions will help your chances of being rescued. Put out a **sea anchor** in order to stay close to the site. When open, the anchor will help to keep the raft in one place. When closed, it will cause the life raft to be pulled along by the current. Signaling and navigation equipment should be carefully protected from the elements, but have them ready to use quickly.

Exercise leadership skills where necessary and give people tasks to do (such as signaler, navigator, spotter, and fisherman). Try to find out who has any specialized skills that might be useful. If you are not the leader, concentrate on carrying out your particular job effectively as best you can. Do not interfere with other people's tasks unless asked. You will be thinking most clearly in the early stages of survival when you are reasonably well fed and watered, so make plans then that you can remember and follow if things become difficult and you become weaker. Put up any permanent signals, such as a flag. Keep a log, recording the prevailing winds,

SWIMMING STROKES FOR SURVIVORS

- Dog paddle: good stroke for when you are clothed or wearing a life jacket.
- Breast stroke: good stroke for swimming underwater or in rough seas.
- Side stroke: a useful stroke to let one arm have a rest.
- Back stroke: gives the arm and chest muscles some relaxation. It is also less tiring because it is easier to float in this position.

During the Vietnam War, SEALs penetrated enemy defenses by floating up river. Together, these teams were called Task Force 116.

weather, currents, and state of the crew on board. This will help in such matters as navigation.

If rescue has not come or if, for any reason, you consider this to be unlikely (it may be that no one knows you are there), then the SEALs say that you should try to find land. There are several signs that may tell you that land is nearby. A stationary cumulus cloud can mean an island nearby. Birds will often be heading toward land in the afternoon and evening. Look out for the particular types of bird and the direction in which they are flying. If it is the morning, they will most likely be heading away from land. A lagoon can create a greenish reflection on the underside of clouds. Floating vegetation and pieces of timber may indicate the proximity of land. Water that is muddy with silt has probably come from the mouth of a large river that is nearby. Deep water is dark green or dark blue; a lighter color indicates shallow water and perhaps land.

Once you have sighted land, your goal is to reach it as soon as possible. If you are swimming, wear your shoes and at least one thickness of clothing. Use side or breast stroke to save your strength. Water is calmer in the sheltered side of a heavy growth of seaweed. Do not swim through it; crawl over the top by grasping the vegetation. Swimming ashore can be difficult because of sea currents and hidden rocks. Yet the SEALs know the right techniques. Ride in on the back of a small wave by swimming forward with it. In high waves, swim toward the shore in the **trough** between waves. Put your face down and submerge yourself beneath the waves, then swim forward in the next trough. If caught beneath a large wave, let it pass over and then push off the bottom with your feet, or swim to the surface if in deep

ABANDONING SHIP

Abandoning ship is a frightening experience, but you must act quickly. Follow these SEAL guidelines and save your life.

- Put on warm, preferably woolen, clothing, including a hat and gloves. Wrap a towel around your neck.
- Take a flashlight.
- Grab chocolates and hard candies if possible.
- Do not inflate your life jacket until you leave the ship.
- When jumping overboard, first throw something (anything wooden) that floats and jump close to it.
- Air trapped in clothing will help buoyancy; do not take off your clothes in the water.

water. When landing on a rocky shore, aim for the place where the waves rush up onto the rocks, not where they explode with a high white spray. To land, advance behind a large wave into the breakers. Face the shore with your feet in front, two to three feet (60–90 cm) lower than your head. In this way, your feet will absorb shocks when you land or hit submerged rocks or reefs, and you will not get injured.

If you do not reach shore behind the wave you have selected, swim using your hands only. Adopt a sitting position as the next wave approaches and carries you to shore. Once ashore, you will need other survival skills. But whether you are on land or at sea, in order to survive you need to know where you are going. Now let the SEALs teach us about navigation at sea and how to signal for help.

This SEAL is lifted to safety by a CH–46D Sea Knight helicopter during training in the Red Sea, May 1996. His kit is suited to surface swimming—short-legged wet suit, mask, fins, and snorkel.

NAVIGATION AND SIGNALING

Seas can be incredibly easy to get lost in. There are no landmarks as there are on the dry land, so you must learn from the SEALs how to find out which direction you are heading in at all times.

If you are in a properly equipped life raft, it should contain navigation equipment with instructions. If you do not have the usual equipment, there are several methods of navigation. The sun can often help you calculate where you are heading. The sun rises in the east and sets in the west. Between sunrise and sunset, you can get a rough estimate of direction by using your watch. Aim the hour hand at the sun. The point halfway between the hour hand and twelve o'clock will show the approximate direction of true south if you are in the northern **hemisphere**, and the approximate direction of true north if you are in the southern hemisphere. However, if you are in the tropics, this method is unreliable because of the dense tree cover.

For night missions, the SEALs are trained to read the stars. The night stars are a reliable guide and have been used by navigators for thousands of years. The most important star in the northern hemisphere is **Polaris** (North Star), which stands over the North Pole. Polaris is part of a faint **constellation** known as **Ursa Minor** (Little Bear), or Little Dipper, and can be identified in the sky by following a line through the two brightest stars of the constellation known as

A U.S. Navy officer plots a course on a naval chart. He uses a pair of dividers and a magnifying lens, and records his actions in a logbook.

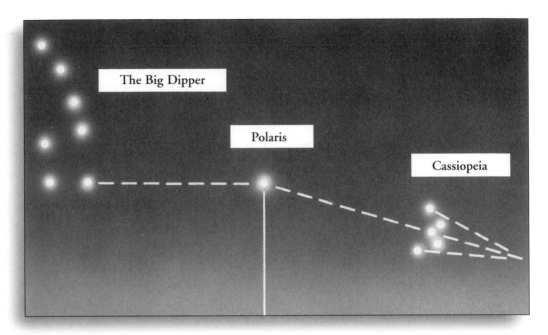

If navigating without a map by night, Polaris, or the North Star, and the Big Dipper, are the best guides for finding the direction of north.

Ursa Major (Great Bear), or Big Dipper. In the southern hemisphere, a constellation known as the **Southern Cross** is used as a guide. The four brightest stars form a cross tilting to the side. Follow the axis of the two furthest apart and continue an imaginary line five times the length of this axis. At about the point where this imaginary line ends, you will find south.

Star movement can be used to determine your position. Watch a star over two fixed points for 15 minutes. You will see it move. In the northern hemisphere, the following rules apply: If the star is rising, you will be facing east. If the star is falling, you will be facing west. If the star is looping to the right, you will be facing south. If the star is looping to the left, you will be facing north. Reverse these rules if you are in the southern hemisphere. The moon can also give you some direction information. If the moon rises before the sun sets, the illuminated side will be on the west. However, if it rises after the sun sets, the illuminated side will be on the east.

When SEALs are at sea, they often carry a large range of signaling equipment with them to attract attention to themselves. If you have them, use flares and dye markers (which spread brightly colored dye in the sea), to attract the attention of a ship or aircraft. If you do not have any signaling equipment, attract attention to yourself by waving clothing and other materials, which are brightly colored if possible. Sea markers should only be used in daylight. (They normally last for around three hours.) A mirror or reflective surface can be used for long-range signaling.

All flares should be handled carefully. Keep them dry and secure, and when firing, point them upward and away from yourself and anyone else in the raft. Use them only when you are sure that they will be seen. A shiny, reflective surface is also an excellent way of attracting attention to yourself. On a sunny day, mirrors, polished canteen cups, belt buckles, or other objects will reflect the sun's rays. Always practice signaling before you need it. Mirror signals can be seen for 62 miles (100 km) under normal conditions and over 100 miles (160 km) in a clear

The Global Positioning System (or GPS) instantly tell SEALs where they are located.

environment. There are several other ways in which you can attract attention to yourself. Many life jackets are fitted with a whistle. Blow the whistle hard to alert boats to your presence. Flashlights or strobe lights can also be seen over great distances.

If aircraft pass overhead, use bold waving actions to attract the crew's attention. Hold a cloth in each hand to make your signals even clearer. Whenever you are making signals, always do so with clear, large movements. (Remember you will be a great distance from the aircraft.) An aircraft that has understood your message will tilt its wings up and down in daylight or make green flashes with its signal lights. If pilots have not understood your message, they will circle their aircraft during daylight or make red flashes with their signal lights at night. Once pilots have received and understood your first message, you can send other messages. Be patient; do not confuse the

When navigating a beach at night, it is important to understand how the beach is structured. The behavior of the offshore, nearshore, foreshore, backshore, and land can make or break a SEAL operation.

person flying the aircraft. Since the ocean is so huge, you might not be found for some days. Survival is going to be tough, but the SEALs are trained to find food and drinking water even in this hostile outdoor environment.

INTERNATIONAL RESCUE CODES

SOS
Pyrotechnics: Red flare.
Auditory signal: 3 short, 3 long, 3 short—repeat every minute.
Light flashes: 3 short, 3 long, 3 short—repeat every minute.

HELP NEEDED
Pyrotechnics: Red flare.
Auditory signal: 6 blasts in quick succession—repeat every minute.
Light flashes: 6 flashes in quick succession—repeat every minute.

MESSAGE UNDERSTOOD
Pyrotechnics: Red flare.
Auditory signal: 3 blasts in quick succession—repeat every minute.
Light flashes: 3 flashes in quick succession—repeat every minute.

FINDING FOOD AND WATER

You are surrounded by water at sea—unfortunately, none of it is drinkable. You must find ways to provide yourself with food and drinking water or you might not survive for more than a few days.

At sea, water is your most precious commodity, as any Navy SEAL will tell you. Do not be tempted to use sea water for drinking or for mixing with fresh water. It is likely to cause vomiting and serious illness. The minimum requirement of fresh drinking water is one pint (475 ml) a day. Follow these water ration rules strictly to increase your chances of survival.

Day 1: Give no water. The body can make use of its own water reserves. Be strict with this rule.
Days 2–4: Give 14 fluid ounces (400 ml) if available.
Day 5 onward: Give two to eight fluid ounces (55–225 ml) daily, depending on water availability and climate.

If you have no way of measuring the fluid, just devise a ration that will give you all a supply of water for over a week, and do not drink for the first 24 hours, or until you have a headache. A big problem is that you lose your body's water through sweating. Follow these

A SEAL is surrounded by water when at sea, but it is not drinkable. In high temperatures, up to three gallons (13.6 liters) is required per day.

SEAL guidelines strictly for reducing your use of body water. In hot climates, reduce sweating by staying still and saving your energy. Brush dried salt off the body with a dry cloth. Try to sleep and rest as much as possible. Try not to get **seasick**. Vomiting causes you to lose valuable fluids. Relax and focus your mind on other tasks. Suck on a button to make saliva and reduce your desire to drink. In a hot climate, keep out of direct sunlight and dampen clothes during the day to keep cool, but do not get overwet or get water in the raft. If there is not enough water, do not eat, because the food will absorb water from your body. In a hot climate, in particular, food is secondary to water. Watch out for rain and make sure you catch it in a tarpaulin and/or other containers. Store as much as possible and always sip water in a slow, steady way to avoid vomiting. Let the body absorb the water rather than overfilling your stomach. Moisten your lips and mouth before swallowing.

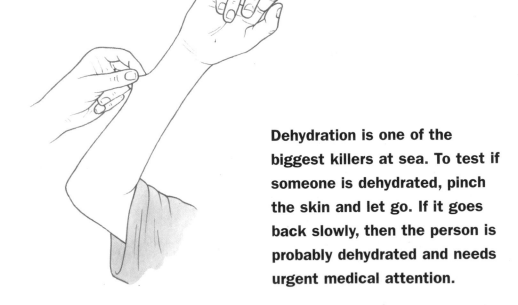

Dehydration is one of the biggest killers at sea. To test if someone is dehydrated, pinch the skin and let go. If it goes back slowly, then the person is probably dehydrated and needs urgent medical attention.

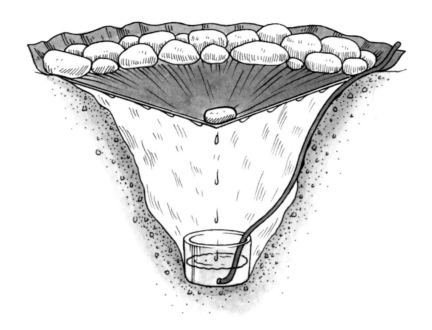

A solar still is a useful method of getting water from the air itself, and can be made at sea if you have the right equipment.

Apart from the rain, there are other ways of finding water. One is a **solar still**. A life raft may be supplied with a solar still. Read the instructions carefully because the still will not work unless the sea is relatively calm. You can also make a solar still by placing a plastic sheet over a container and securing it with whatever is on hand. Place coins or a stone in the center of the sheet. In the morning, the sun raises the overall temperature of the air to produce vapor. Water then condenses on the underside of the sheet and runs down into the container.

Icebergs provide a source of water in cold climates. Old sea ice will have lost much of its saltiness, but new ice will taste unpleasant. Old ice can be recognized by its smooth shapes and blue color. Do not approach large or moving icebergs, since these may crush the life raft or overturn it suddenly.

Some of the water from inland icebergs is edible. The blue color indicates that the ice has lost much of its ocean saltiness.

It is advisable to eat nothing for as long as possible and remember not to eat too much if little water is available. However, food will be essential if you are to survive for a few days. When it comes to finding food, fish are the obvious choice for SEALs. Fish will be your main food source. Flying fish may even jump into your raft! In the open sea, without land in sight, fish are generally safe to eat. However, do not eat fish that are brightly colored, covered with bristles or spines, or those which puff up or have parrotlike mouths or teeth like humans. Also, avoid fish eggs in clusters or clumps; these will be poisonous. Catching fish is not easy if you are improvising. Yet the SEALs are expert fishermen as well as expert soldiers. Follow their advice for safe fishing.

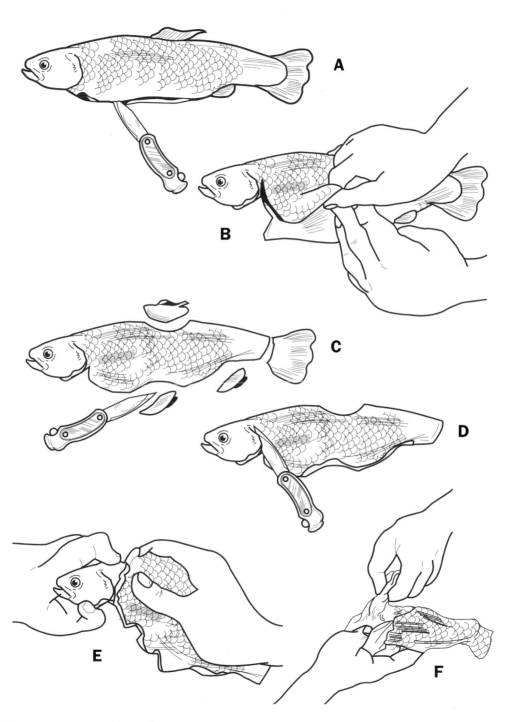

The process of gutting and preparing fresh fish or shellfish can be done swiftly and cleanly with a sharp knife.

Do not touch the fishing line with your bare hands when reeling in, and never wrap it around your hands or tie it to an inflatable dinghy. The salt on it makes a sharp cutting edge that is a danger to your hands and the raft. If you have gloves, wear them when handling fish; that way, you will not get fins or fish teeth in your skin. Pass a net under your raft from one end to the other—fish and turtles are attracted to the shade under your raft. (You need at least two people to perform this.) Use a flashlight to attract fish at night. Make improvised hooks from small pieces of wire and small bright objects.

Use the guts of a fish, or **organ meats**, that you have caught previously or a small fish as bait to catch larger fish (though they can also be used as food). Cut loose any fish that are too large to handle and do not fish if sharks may be near. Head for large shoals of fish, but remember that shark and barracuda may also be present. Be careful not to puncture the dinghy with the fish hooks. You can also bind a knife to an oar to use as a spear to catch fish.

Experiment with different ways of fishing and find out what works best for you. Once you have caught a fish, you should gut it immediately. (See the diagram on page 51.) This is not pleasant, but it has to be done. Slit the fish with your knife from the anus to just behind the gills (A) and pull out the internal organs (B). Clean the flesh, then cut off the fins and tail (C). Cut down to, but not through, the spine. Cut around the spine, finishing behind the gills on both sides (D). Insert your thumb along the top of the spine and begin to pull it away from the flesh (E). The ribs should come out cleanly with the spine (F). Eat the fish raw.

TREATING SEASICKNESS

Seasickness cannot be taken lightly: it can seriously weaken sufferers and lower the morale of other survivors. Deal with it the way that U.S. Navy SEALs do.

- Wash the patient and raft to remove the sight and smell of vomit.
- Do not let patient have any food until nausea or sickness has passed.
- Make the patient lie down and rest.
- If available, administer seasickness pills.
- Try to get the patient to focus on something other than the sickness, such as steering the boat or fishing.

The SEALs will also show you that fish are not all that you can eat at sea. All seabirds are edible, for example. They will be attracted to your raft as a perching place. Wait until they land on your raft, then try to grab them before they fly away. However, the best method is to use a hook covered in fish, which can be trailed behind the boat. The hook gets stuck in seabirds' throat. Use a noose or net, similarly camouflaged, to trap their legs.

Some seaweeds can also be eaten. They should be eaten only if they are firm to the touch and odorless. Do not eat slender, branched varieties of seaweed. These contain acids that will make you feel ill. Make sure that there are no sea creatures attached to the seaweed before eating it. You can collect seaweed around shorelines and in mid-ocean. Remember that seaweed absorbs fluids when your body is digesting it, so it should not be eaten when water is scarce. You should eat only small amounts of seaweed at a time, because it can cause you to have bowel movements or need to urinate, losing more precious water from your body.

If fish, birds, and seaweed are not enough for survival, then a SEAL will also eat **plankton**. Plankton consists of tiny plants and animals that drift around or swim weakly in the oceans. They can be caught by dragging a net through the water. Plankton contains many nutrients, yet it can make you ill when eaten in large quantities. If you are living solely on plankton, therefore, you must

Seabirds can be caught by attaching a fish or other bait to a hook, dragging it behind the boat, then securing with a makeshift net.

eat small quantities at first. In addition, you should ensure you have an adequate supply of drinking water; digesting plankton will use up your body fluids. Each plankton catch should be thoroughly checked before you eat it: remove all jellyfish tentacles (be careful not to get stung), discard the plankton that have become jelly-like, and check for species that are spiny. If the catch contains large amounts of spiny plankton, you can dry or crush it before eating.

As you can see, it is possible to live off the sea even when you are miles away from land. However, the sea is also a cruel place to be. The SEALs will now teach you what dangers to avoid.

LIFE RAFT CONTENTS

Soldiers stranded at sea will stand a much better chance of finding food, not to mention being rescued if they have access to a professional life raft. Contents you might find in a life raft include the following:

Sea anchor	Paddles
First-aid kit	Fishing line
Bellows	Survival leaflets
Bailer	Repair kit
Flares	Knife
Sponge	Fresh water
Eating equipment	Can opener
Seasickness pills	Flashlight

DANGERS

The sea is home to some of the world's most dangerous creatures, including sharks, lethal poisonous fish, and massive killer whales. Knowing how to avoid these animals can save your life.

The first dangerous sea creature most people think of is a shark. Sharks are scavengers and live in almost all seas and oceans. They feed more actively at night, and especially at dawn and dusk. After dark, they move toward the surface and into shallow waters. They are attracted to garbage, body wastes, and blood, and also by weak splashing movements similar to those of a wounded fish. A shark cannot stop suddenly or turn quickly in a tight circle, and it will rarely jump out of the water to take food. For this reason, people on rafts are safe unless they dangle their legs or arms in the water.

The main types of shark that have been known to attack humans are listed below, but be aware that all sharks, because of their sharp teeth and aggressive feeding habits, must be considered potentially dangerous. One more thing: there is no relationship between the size of a shark and the risk of attack.

Nurse shark
Appearance: gray on top, white underneath, very heavily built, and large-finned.

Even with protective clothing, SEALs are at risk from a variety of ocean animals, including sharks, poisonous sea snakes, and jellyfish.

Sharks are one of the world's most lethal killers. They have a primal instinct to ruthlessly hunt down prey, which is why they are the SEALs' most feared enemy. The nurse shark (above) can be aggressive toward swimmers, which is a significant factor for Navy SEALs when planning inshore operations.

Length: around 13 feet (4 m). *Weight:* 640 pounds (290 kg).

Temperament and habits: aggressive, often found close inshore.

Distribution: around eastern Australia.

Hammerhead shark

Appearance: flat, hammerlike head, long body.

Length: up to 18 feet (5.4 m). *Weight:* 880 pounds (400 kg).

Temperament: can be aggressive.

Distribution: tropical and subtropical waters.

Tiger shark

Appearance: gray on top, white underneath with a very wide head and jaws.

Shark-finned submarines are ideal for covert missions, since they enable SEALs to move undetected in enemy waters.

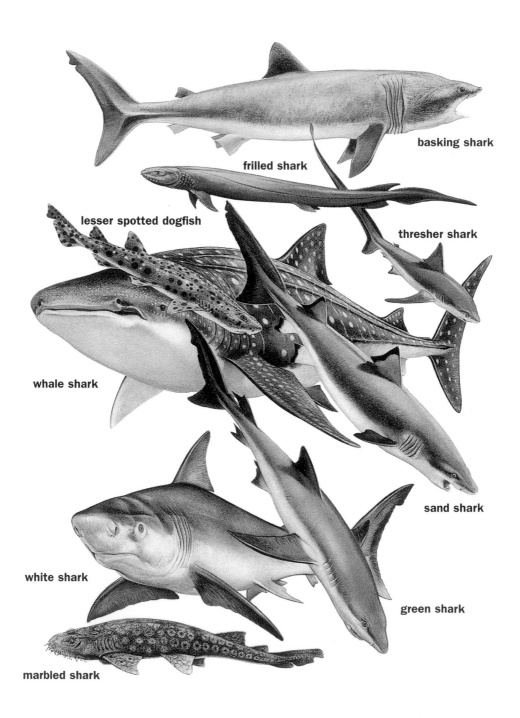

basking shark

frilled shark

thresher shark

lesser spotted dogfish

whale shark

sand shark

white shark

green shark

marbled shark

These are the some of the main shark species. Remember, the biggest are not necessarily the most dangerous. Some of the small ones, such as the sand shark, are easily provoked to attack.

Length: 12–13$^{1}/_{2}$ feet (3.6–3.4 m). *Weight:* 1,900 pounds (870 kg).
Temperament and habits: often found close inshore, can be dangerous.
Distribution: tropical and subtropical waters.

Mako shark

Appearance: bright blue on top and creamy white underneath. Brightly colored.
Length: six to nine feet (1.8–2.7 m). *Weight:* 1,115 pounds (500 kg).
Temperament and habits: can swim very quickly, and sometimes leaps from the water when agitated.
Distribution: warm **temperate** waters.

Great white shark

Appearance: gray on top, white underneath, thick body, conical snout, and black eyes.
Length: up to 18 feet (6 m). *Weight:* 7,500 pounds (3,400 kg).
Temperament: very aggressive.
Distribution: found in all the warm and temperate oceans of the world, but especially off southern Africa, east and west of North America, and southern Australia and New Zealand.

Cow shark

Appearance: sandy gray with dark spots.
Length: up to nine feet (2.7 m). *Weight:* 1,300 pounds (590 kg).
Temperament and habits: swims close to the surface, aggressive.
Distribution: tropical and subtropical waters.

Sand shark

Appearance: white underneath, gray on top with yellow spots, hence its name.

Length: up to nine feet (2.7 m). *Weight:* 340 pounds (155 kg).

Temperament and habits: aggressive when provoked.

Distribution: tropical and subtropical waters.

Snaggletooth

Appearance: golden brown or gray in color.

Length: six feet (1.8 m). *Weight:* 75 pounds (35 kg).

Temperament and habits: can be found in shallow waters, can be aggressive.

Distribution: tropical waters.

Silvertip shark

Appearance: charcoal-colored, white tips on fins.

Length: nine feet (2.7 m). *Weight:* 183 pounds (83 kg).

Temperament and habits: fast and bold, potentially dangerous. Plentiful around reefs and islands.

Distribution: tropical and subtropical waters.

Gray reef shark

Appearance: gray, tail edged with black.

Length: six feet (1.8 m). *Weight:* 75 pounds (34 kg).

Temperament and habits: curious but not aggressive.

Distribution: tropical waters.

Copper shark

Appearance: golden brown on top and cream underneath.
Length: 10 feet (3 m). *Weight:* 500 pounds (227 kg).
Temperament and habits: can be very aggressive.
Distribution: tropical and subtropical waters.

Bull shark

Appearance: gray on top, off-white underneath.
Length: $11^{1}/_{2}$ feet (3.5 m). *Weight:* 670 pounds (305 kg).

These SEAL divers investigate the submerged submarine, *Woodrow Wilson*, Puerto Rico, 1991. Divers traditionally work in buddy pairs, and are often joined by a length of rope to maintain contact.

Temperament and habits: dangerous—this is the most feared of tropical sharks.

Distribution: the tropics; will swim up rivers.

Blue shark

Appearance: brilliant blue on top, white underneath.

Length: 13 feet (4 m). *Weight:* 440 pounds (200 kg).

Temperament and habits: one of the most dangerous sharks in the ocean; responsible for many human fatalities and injuries.

Distribution: world-wide in tropical and temperate waters.

Beware of all sharks and try to ensure that you do not draw their attention. Sharks can be found in every ocean and sea, and can sense movement as well as blood and other decaying matter, such as vomit. Remember that not all fish you see with fins are sharks. For example, dolphins and **porpoises** can resemble sharks, and are no threat to humans.

Here's the SEALs advice for avoiding sharks: Treat seasickness as soon as possible to avoid putting vomit in the water. If you do need to get rid of vomit, throw it as far away as possible behind the raft, so that the current sweeps it away. Try to limit the amount of urine or excrement that goes into the water at any one time. If you are cut or have been bitten, stop the bleeding as soon as possible. If on a dinghy or raft, do not dangle your limbs under the water. Like most **predators**, sharks will normally attack an animal that is showing signs of weakness. So if you are attacked, shout, slap the water, kick, or rap or poke the shark with a stick. These actions

Sharks are attracted to surfers or swimmers using body boards; they confuse them with seals, which are one of their favorite meals.

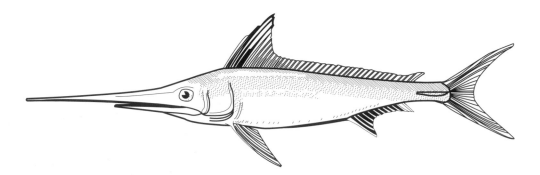

Swordfish are aggressive only if provoked. The sharp, pointed spike on the upper jaw can easily puncture a life raft or cause injury.

may be enough to persuade it to turn elsewhere. If there are other people in the water, huddle together facing outward, and beat the water with strong regular strokes. The shark will sense the confidence of your movements. Let your **adrenaline** fuel your anger and not your fear.

Unfortunately, sharks are not the only problem in the sea. There are many other types of poisonous sea creatures you need to avoid at all costs. If in doubt, never eat a fish you are not sure about. Fish poisons are tasteless, and no amount of cooking will make the fish safe. In addition, birds can be immune to these poisons. Just because you see a bird eating a fish, do not think that it is safe for you to eat it as well.

Eating poisonous fish can result in death in the worst cases. As soon as any symptoms arise—numbness, itching, or sickness—get the person to vomit by giving saltwater to drink. There are other fish that are dangerous to touch, either because they have venomous spines, such as stonefish, or because they have poisonous barbs in their tails, such as rays. The spines inject a **venom** that is excruciatingly painful. Keep your shoes or boots on at all times when you are walking through saltwater, and use a stick, not your hands, to explore sand, rocks, and holes.

The main types of dangerous sea creature that the SEALs can recognize are listed here.

Auger or tenebra shell

These are slightly narrower than cone shells (see next page), and although their poison is less powerful, it is still very dangerous.

Blue-ringed octopus

These are deadly poisonous. Grayish white with blue, ringlike marks, blue-ringed octopuses are native to the Australian barrier **reef**. The poison they secrete is so powerful that it can kill prey even without contact.

Although only eight inches (20 cm) long, the blue-ringed octopus delivers a deadly poison. It is found among coral and rock pools.

Cone shell (right)

Widely distributed in the Pacific and Indian Oceans, cone shells are very poisonous. They store up poison in a duct which is several times longer than the fish itself and inject it through a needle.

Moray eels

Powerful predators, they rest during the day, becoming active at night. They are common in warm tropical waters and have a dangerous bite. Adults can grow to five feet (1.5 m).

Portuguese man-of-war

Common in tropical water, especially off the Florida coast, it drifts in surface water, catching unwary fish in its tentacles. The tentacles, which can be 40 feet (12 m) long, contain stinging cells that can be fatal to humans.

Puffer fish

There are hundreds of varieties of this tropical fish. The delicately mottled Japanese variety is poisonous when eaten.

When alarmed or threatened, the puffer fish inflates its chest.

Rabbitfish (right)
Rabbitfish are quite similar to sharks in their body structure, with five gill slits They live and feed on the bottom of the ocean. The spine of the dorsal fin is very poisonous.

Rockfish, scorpionfish, lionfish
Saltwater fishes characterized by massive bodies and large heads armored with spines that inject poison that is sometimes lethal.

Sea snakes
Sea snakes are deadly poisonous. They are unlikely to bite, but stay well clear of them.

Stingray
Found in warm, shallow waters, stingrays use their dorsal fin as a highly poisonous spike. They have flattened and very extended bodies in which the tail is reduced to a defensive whip. They live and feed in sandy and muddy areas on the ocean bed. Sometimes they ascend rivers and into fresh water.

Stonefish
Any of several small, spiny venomous scorpion fish common about coral reefs of the Indian and Pacific Oceans. Their natural camouflage makes them resemble stones or rocks. They dig themselves into the sea bed, making them almost impossible to see. Their sting is very painful and can be fatal.

There are over 200 species of jellyfish, and many swim in shallow waters. Short-legged wet suits are ideal for warm water operations, but do not protect the legs from multiple stings.

Tang or surgeonfish

Tropical water fish with brightly colored markings. Surgeonfish get their name because of the presence of sharp, flat spines located on either side of the tail base that can inflict sharp cuts and are reminiscent of a surgeon's scalpel.

Toadfish

Toadfish live among the seaweed of rocky coasts of warm seas. They have poisonous spines on the dorsal fins and gill covers. They have broad heads, large mouths, and strong teeth which give off a powerful bite if touched.

Triggerfish

Poisonous. When threatened, they can lock themselves in between rocks with the aid of their fins and cannot be pulled out.

Tuna

Potentially dangerous. The commonest tuna is the bluefin tuna which can grow to 15 feet (4.5 m) in length and attain a weight of 1,800 pounds (800 kg).

In general, SEALs are careful of fish that inhabit lagoons and reefs, and in particular of fish with small, parrotlike mouths and small belly fins. Yet the most common type of dangerous sea creature is the jellyfish. There are many different kinds of jellyfish. The largest can be six feet (1.8 m) in diameter, with tentacles hanging down to a depth of up to 100 feet (30 m).

These tentacles contain stinging cells that can inflict serious injury on the survivor. One of the deadliest is the sea wasp, which can cause death in as little as 30 seconds, though around three hours is normal.

Steer clear of all jellyfish, especially since their tentacles may trail a long way from their body. Following a storm in tropical areas where large numbers of jellyfish are present, you may be stung by pieces of floating tentacles that have been broken off the jellyfish during the storm. Jellyfish washed up on a shore may look dead, but many can still inflict painful injuries. In general, try to get out of the water when jellyfish are present.

Other types of stinging creature include marine snails and slugs. As a survivor, you may come into contact with these when you are crossing coral reefs and sandy shores. You should avoid them; they can inject poison by plunging a barb into your flesh. The sting made by a cone shell is a puncture-type wound. When you are stung, the area

The world's largest octopus is the North Pacific octopus, which grows up to 30 feet (9 m) long and weighs 150 pounds (68 kg).

around the wound will turn blue, swell, become numb, sting, and burn. The degree of pain varies from person to person, though in all victims the numbness and tingling sensation around the wound quickly spreads through the whole body. This can be followed in a matter of hours by complete paralysis and death. There is no specific treatment for this kind of injury. The best that you can do is apply hot towels or soak the wound in hot water to relieve the pain.

All SEALs are taught to respect the wildlife of the sea. The general rule is, if you stay away from dangerous sea creatures, they will be more likely to stay away from you.

DEALING WITH JELLYFISH STINGS

A jellyfish sting can be extremely painful, and in extreme cases can be fatal. Follow these SEALs guidelines for dealing with them.

- Get the victim out of the water as soon as possible because jellyfish stings may result in life-threatening convulsions.
- Remove tentacles or other bits of the jellyfish from the skin immediately, using clothing, seaweed, or other material.
- Do not rub the wound with anything, especially sand, because this may worsen the sting.
- Do not suck the wound.
- Try to stop the poisoning effects; try putting soap, lemon juice, plant juices, baking powder, or even urine on it.

RAFTS AND SAILING

If you need to survive at sea, a good raft will improve your chances. The U.S. Navy SEALs use modern boats, but they can also build seagoing rafts from the most basic materials if necessary.

If you are the survivor of a boat or aircraft disaster, there's a good chance that you will have an inflatable raft. Getting into these rafts from the water can be tricky. If the raft is attached to you with a rope, pull the raft toward you. Then grab handles on each side of the raft and pull yourself in, while kicking with your legs in the water. Another way of boarding is to get one knee inside the raft and pull yourself forward into it. When you are in the raft, make sure it is fully inflated, then check for any leaks.

You must remember one thing when afloat in the ocean: your raft will be at the mercy of winds and currents. Sea currents travel at speeds of less than five miles per hour (8 km/h), so movement is very slow. In areas where warm and cold currents meet, there will often be storms, dense fog, high winds, and heavy seas. These will make movement difficult and dangerous. Winds and waves can aid raft travel. To take advantage of the wind, you will need a sail. If the raft does not have one, make one from a piece of material.

Waves can be both helpful and dangerous. The size of waves is dependent upon the strength of the wind. Waves will move a raft

SEALs are adept at using standard issue Navy life rafts, but in an emergency, they must be able to construct one from found objects.

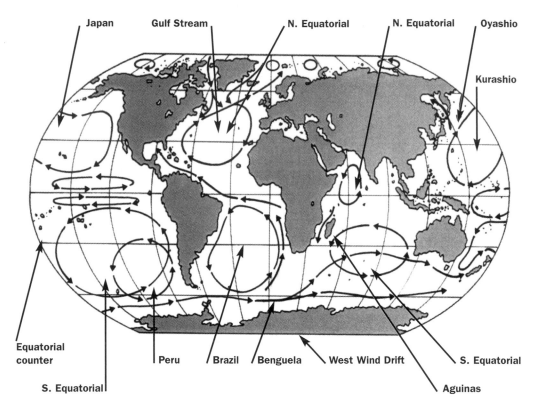

Currents are affected by wind, the ocean's salinity, and heat. Knowing how currents work can help you navigate if you are lost at sea.

only a few inches (several centimeters) at a time under normal conditions, so you will not move fast. Waves are useful indicators if you are searching for shallow areas or land. Ocean waves break when they enter shallow water or when they encounter an obstruction. Use breaking waves as an aid to making a landfall. Waves can also capsize a raft in bad weather, or fill it with water.

All SEALs know how to make rafts if professional boats are not available. Rafts are better for river travel, but they can also be used for short sea journeys, such as traveling between islands in the tropics. Some small rafts, such as the brush raft, can be constructed very easily, though they are not recommended for lengthy travel. Rafts will not capsize easily if they are made properly, but you must remember the following points before setting out on your journey:

• Test your raft soundly in safe water before setting out.

• Tie all equipment securely to the raft or to the safety line. All survivors should have a rope tied around their waists and be secured to the raft.

The simplest raft for one person is the log flotation raft, for which you need two logs of light wood. Place the logs side by side about two feet (60 cm) apart and tie them together securely. You will then be able to

Before using a raft on the ocean, SEALs are trained in its use in the safety of a swimming pool, guided by qualified instructors.

Since SEALs often approach land in inflatable boats, they must perfect their ship-to-ship skills with the host carrier.

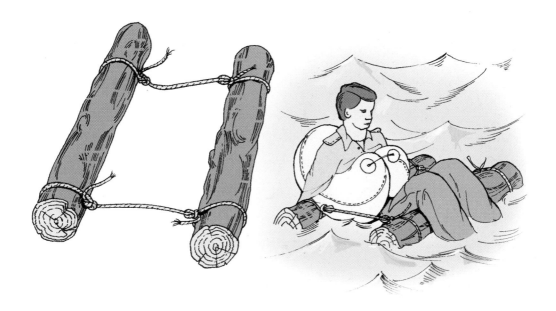

If securely built, a log flotation raft can keep you afloat for a few hours, but it is not a long-term survival solution.

float on them. Another easy raft to build is a vegetation raft. This is made out of small vegetation that will float. Place the plants in material or clothing to form a raft for equipment or people. (It will not hold heavy weights, though.)

If you have rope available, you can construct a simple log raft. Tie the logs securely together using the rope. Place two or more logs underneath running at right angles to the logs above. This gives your raft strength. Remember to cut notches into the logs and make sure the ropes run along them. These notches will stop the ropes from slipping over the logs once you are out at sea.

Landing a raft can be one of the most dangerous moments. If the land is likely to have people living there, send a signal and wait for rescuers to come out to you. If you have to make a landing, choose your position carefully. Keep clear of rocks or strong surf. Look for gaps in the surf line. Go to the sheltered side of the island, where you will be protected from the wind. Strong tides may wash you back out to sea, so try to spot find a sloping beach where the surf is less strong.

You may be carried along parallel to the beach and some distance out to sea by a **rip current**, or riptide. This is a surge of seawater escaping from the beach. Do not try to swim or paddle directly against the current. Swim or paddle along with the rip current for a short distance to allow its force to dissipate. Then head back in toward the shore. Beware of coral reefs in the Pacific—they will be difficult to see from low down in the water. Keep looking out for gaps.

Even if you have a good raft, it does not mean that you are safe. Living at sea can make you ill, so it is important that you know a few essential first-aid techniques used by the SEALs.

RIGHTING A CAPSIZED DINGHY

A capsized dinghy need not be a catastrophe in a survival situation at sea; you can right it easily if you know how.

- Grab the righting line from the opposite side.
- Brace your feet against the dinghy and pull.
- The dinghy should rise up and over, and will pull you temporarily out of the water.
- This procedure requires more effort in heavy seas or high winds.

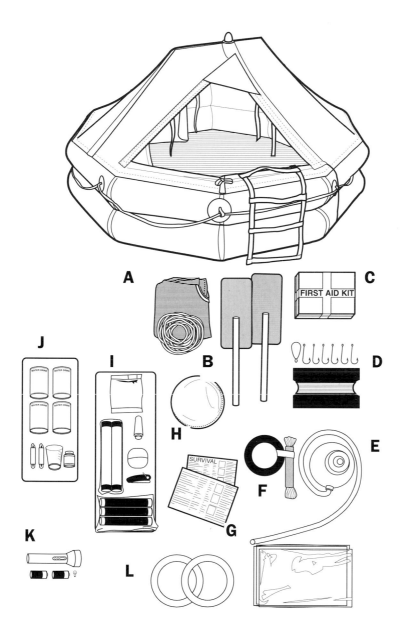

The contents of a four-person life raft: sea anchor (A), paddles (B), first-aid kit (C), fishing line and hooks (D), bellow (E), quoit and line (F), survival leaflets (G), bailer (H), repair kit, flares, sponge, knife (I), water, can opener, cup, seasickness pills (J), flashlight and batteries (K), and resealing lids (L).

FIRST AID

Out in the ocean, there are few doctors on call. That is why the SEALs are experts in delivering survival first aid. Prompt attention to injuries and illnesses is needed to stop simple problems from becoming life threatening.

Even for tough SEALs, the greatest danger when you are surviving at sea is exposure to the elements. In a raft, do not expose yourself to the sun and wind needlessly. A SEAL will keep a layer of clothing on at all times, especially on the head. If you are very hot, dip your clothing in the sea, then wring it out and put it back on. Place any injured persons on the floor of the raft and make them comfortable. Try to keep them as warm or cool (depending on where you are), and as dry as possible.

Wear sunglasses or eye shields to protect your eyes from the glare of the sun. Be particularly careful about reflection off the water, which intensifies the sun's rays. Do not rub sore eyes; apply an **antiseptic** cream (if you have it) to the eye lids and bandage them lightly instead.

For parched lips and cracked skin, apply sunblock or Vaseline and do not lick your lips. Cover dry skin to prevent it becoming even dryer. Try to keep your clothing as dry as possible. Clean any sore that develops with fresh water and apply antiseptic cream.

An injured SEAL is carried aboard the amphibious assault ship, *U.S.S. Wasp,* after being saved by a search and rescue team.

Large sores should be covered with a bandage, but change the bandages regularly.

Sunburns are very common problem in sea survival. Even in the hottest climates, make sure that vulnerable skin is well covered. A sunburn can become a serious problem because it can lead to badly blistered, painful, and infected skin. As with all burns, do not burst any blisters. The best treatment is to use cold compresses (water-soaked material applied to the wound and re-soaked regularly to keep it chilled) for around 10 minutes. Also provide the victim with cold water to drink. Most importantly, get the victim into shelter—make one out of material if need be.

Sometimes blisters can disable a large area of flesh. On the whole, do not burst them, because blisters form to help skin heal and keep out infection. However, there can be exceptions. If the blister stops the victim from moving easily, then you might have to break it. In this case bursting can be done through the following technique:

- Clean the area around the blister thoroughly using fresh water and soap if you have it. (Never use drinking water if you haven't got enough to spare.)
- Use a **sterilized** needle or blade to pierce the blister. Sterilization can be achieved by immersing the steel in alcohol, boiling it for about five minutes, or holding it over a flame. Even better would be to have sterilized needles sealed away in a medical pack.
- Pierce the blister at one end and let the fluid drain out. Do not pull away the blistered skin. Instead, let it stay there to protect the wound from infection.

A soldier stranded at sea is vulnerable to heat stroke, sunburn, dehydration, hypothermia (exposure to cold), and frostbite. For frostbite, it is important to thaw the affected areas and keep them dry.

SEALs must take precautions to protect their fellow team members and avoid diving injuries, such as damage to the ear canal or lungs.

• Cover the wound and clean it regularly. Keep checking to see if it is infected and apply some antibiotic ointment if you have it.

We have already seen that the sea is home to many of the world's most poisonous creatures. Knowing how to treat the injuries that these can give is an important part of SEAL training. Poisonous sea creatures deliver their venom in a variety of ways. Mostly they do it using poisonous spines, such as are found on stingrays and sea urchins. Or the poison is delivered by something called **nematocysts**. These are the stinging parts of creatures like jellyfish, anemones, and octopuses. They inject lots of tiny stinging cells, which stick themselves into the skin.

To treat spine poison, clean the wound with water, but be wary of any stinging bits stuck to the skin. Take these out carefully with

If caught in a shoal of jellyfish, swim slowly through them, being careful not to let them touch your skin.

tweezers. Treat this type of wound with heat. Place the wounded area in hot water, as hot as the victim can bear, for up to 90 minutes. The pain should slowly go away.

Nematocyst toxin is different because the poison stays on the skin to keep stinging. It should be washed off with large amounts of saltwater (not fresh water, which will only worsen stinging). Once this is done, scrape the sting site downward with a solid, flat object such as the back of a knife. If you can, soak the wound with vinegar for about 30 minutes to neutralize the stings. Following this, coat the wound in a powder (such as talcum), before brushing the talcum powder off, taking with it the remaining nematocysts. This is how the SEALs might deal with poisonous injuries.

One final injury deserves a mention for the sea survivor—how to get fish hooks out of the skin. This is difficult because the hooks are designed to stay embedded. If you have to remove one, cut it away

Diving descent is always risky, because the increased water pressure can cause a dangerous vacuum to build up inside the mask or suit.

RESCUING A DROWNING PERSON

A drowning person usually goes into a blind panic, so unless the victim is in shallow water or you have been trained in water rescue techniques, do not be tempted to go in after them. It is better that you stay on the bank and throw them a buoyancy aid or a length of rope with which to pull them in. If you are forced to enter the water, take a buoyancy aid with you and give it to the victim upon reaching them. Try to calm the victim as much as possible.

from the line and, if you have wire cutters, cut the barb (the sharp pronged piece at the end) as well. Once the barb is removed, hold the eye of the hook and take it back following the shape of the hook. If you haven't got wire cutters, or the barb is embedded in the skin, then you have to push the barb forward and through the skin. Take hold of it with a cloth or other protective material, and withdraw it with the eye coming through last. This can be a painful procedure for the victim, so do it with a decisive, steady action until it is completed. Then dress the wound with a bandage.

Most problems at sea can be avoided by being careful in the first place. As we have seen, even though they are tough soldiers, the U.S. Navy SEALs still have a lot of respect for the sea. By treating the sea with caution and care, disasters are much less likely to happen and they will not have to use their survival skills. This is the best situation of all.

GLOSSARY

Adrenaline A chemical released into your body when you are excited or afraid, which gives you great strength.

Amphibious Able to operate/live on both land and water.

Antiseptic Something is antiseptic when it acts to kill germs and bacteria on wounds and injuries.

Atmosphere The air and other gases that surround our planet.

Constellation A group of stars in the night sky, which are given a single name.

Dinghy An inflatable rubber life raft.

Exposure A dangerous medical problem that happens when a person exposed to the weather becomes colder than is safe.

Flak The name for explosive artillery shells that are fired at aircraft.

HELP A word that stands for Heat Escaping Lessing Posture, a special way of swimming that stops you from losing too much body heat in the water.

Hemisphere One half of the Earth. The Earth is usually divided into the northern and southern hemispheres at the equator.

Nematocysts Stinging cells on some sea creatures, such as jellyfish, which give a painful, burning sting when touched.

North Vietnamese Army The communist army of North Vietnam, which fought against South Vietnam and the United States in the Vietnam War.

Mare's tails Another name for cirrus clouds, which are long and feathery.

Organ meats The body organs from inside an animal, such as the heart, intestines, and liver.

Plankton Tiny plants and creatures that float in huge numbers around the world's seas, oceans, and rivers.

Polaris Another name for the North Star, which always points to the north and is useful for navigation.

Porpoises Small whales with fins, rather like a dolphin or shark.

Predators Anything that preys on other animals for its food.

Reef A ridge of rock, sand, or coral just beneath the surface of the waves, which is dangerous to boats.

Rip current A strong current that flows across the top of the water and can drag a swimmer back out to sea.

Safe house A secret place in which a person in danger is able to hide.

Scud A long-range missile used a lot by Iraq during the Gulf War.

Sea anchor A hollow cone of material dragged behind a boat to either hold it it one place or drag it along with the current.

Seasick The feeling of sickness that can occur when tossed around by waves.

Smart bombs Bombs that actually fly straight to their target after they have been dropped. They are guided by laser beams.

Solar still A simple device for collecting dew and water vapor to use for drinking water.

Southern Cross A group of stars in the southern hemisphere, which point directly south.

Sterilized Cleaned of germs and dirt.

Temperate A region where the temperatures are mild.

Trough The flat, low stretch of water between two waves.

Ursa Major One of the biggest constellations in the northern hemisphere, also known as the Great Bear.

Ursa Minor A constellation in the northern hemisphere, also know as the Little Bear, which contains the North Star.

Venom Poison injected by poisonous animals.

Viet Cong The communist guerrilla soldiers that the U.S. Navy SEALs fought against in the Vietnam War.

Waterspouts Tornadoes at sea that drag huge columns of water into the air.

RECRUITMENT INFORMATION

To enter SEAL training, you must pass a rigorous physical test, especially of your swimming, and also do well in the Armed Services Vocational Aptitude Battery (ASVAB) intelligence test. You must be a U.S. citizen and up to 28 years old. The initial fitness test involves a series of exercises punctuated by short rests:

- 500-yard (500-m) swim using breast and/or sidestroke in $12^{1}/_{2}$ minutes. 10-minute rest.
- Perform a minimum of 42 push-ups in two minutes. Two-minute rest.
- Perform a minimum of 50 sit-ups in two minutes. Two-minute rest.
- Perform a minimum of six chin-ups (there is no time limit). Ten-minute rest.
- Run a mile and a half (2.4 km) wearing boots and long pants in $11^{1}/_{2}$ minutes.

If you pass this, you then go on to Basic Underwater Demolitions/SEAL training (BUDS). This is one of the toughest training courses in the world, and up to 80 percent of people fail. It can last up to one year and trains you in every form of combat, but especially underwater/marine missions. There are three main phases to BUDS: basic conditioning (9 weeks), diving (7 weeks), and demolitions and land warfare (9 weeks). If you do go for the SEALs, make sure that you are very fit before you start!

There are 2,300 qualified SEALs currently in service.

To find out more about the SEALs entry requirements and training go to:
http://www.sealchallenge.navy.mil
http://www.navyseals.com
http://www.chinfo.navy.mil
http://www.defenselink.mil